BEYOND BROKENNESS...

A LOVE THAT WOULD NOT LET GO

BEYOND BROKENNESS...

A LOVE THAT WOULD NOT LET GO

KIMBERLY ROBERTS LIVINGSTON

XULON PRESS

Xulon Press
2301 Lucien Way #415
Maitland, FL 32751
407.339.4217
www.xulonpress.com

Paperback ISBN-13: 978-1-66281-888-2

IT WAS 2003 WHEN THE FIRST THOUGHT OF WRITING this book came to me; little did I know eighteen years later, it would become reality. In 2005, while attending a church ladies' conference, it was prophesied by the speaker to me that I would write a book. I had told no one at the time about writing a book. While lying in the bed about three years later, God gave me the title, but it was not until 2013 I would pick up a pen and paper and begin to write the book you are holding in your hands.

This book seemed beyond my ability and out of reach many times. Why me? I am only a common girl with a life of scars. Why me?... Because of three words....GOD KEPT ME. He kept me for you. God's plan is bigger than we can see, beyond our abilities to accomplish, and almost always is a path we would never have chosen to walk.

**Beyond Brokenness...A Love That Would Not Let Go** is the story of a young girl that through insecurities, fears, rejection, divorce, and abandonment found there was a love not from family, friend, or a man, but from a heavenly Father who never let go of her, even though she let go many times. I promise we will laugh, cry, and roll our eyes as we go through the next pages together. My prayer is when you have read the last word, you will know there is a love beyond your earthly understanding that will hold you tight through the process called life. He never promised us a pain-free life; He did promise HE would never leave or forsake us.

Let's get started...

As a young girl, all I ever wanted was to be a wife, mother, and to work for the Lord. I grew up a child of divorce, as my parents divorced when my mother was five months pregnant with me. My mother, sister, and I lived with her parents after the divorce, and even though I grew up in a loving, stable Christian home with anything I wanted, there was always an emptiness in my life because of a missing father. My grandfather filled the position of father and grandfather, and I was always a "Papaw's girl" and fought for him until the day he passed in 2014.

One of my fondest memories was when I turned ten years old and he took me to a new toy store that had opened in our city's mall. I got to pick out whatever toy I wanted, so I chose the Tic Tac Toe board game. My grandfather and I had such a special bond between us, but the emptiness of not having my father in my life was very real. I recall going to town and passing men, wondering *Is that my dad? Wonder what he looks like.*

The only thing I had from my dad was a green stuffed frog, a set of encyclopedias, and a globe, which he sent to my sister and I through our cousin when we were in middle school. I do not remember seeing pictures of him, and he was never talked about by Mom or my grandparents.

Growing up without a father left a hole in my life that no one could fill; but only one person could ever heal this hole, and that's God. I was always searching for a love to fill the rejection from my father, which caused problems in other relationships. The feelings of rejection started here in my life with thoughts like, *Why would my father not want to be around his own daughter? Maybe it was my fault my parents divorced?* The only thing I knew was my mom was pregnant with me, so in my mind, it had to be something to do with me. No one would ever talk about the divorce so all I had to form the reasons for the divorce were the thoughts in my own mind. Right or wrong, these thoughts were all I had to go on to start forming an image of myself.

So, I always thought something had to be wrong with me. As years passed, the thoughts grew to, *If my dad left me, then I know no boy will ever want me either. I'm not pretty, tall, skinny, or smart like the other girls.* I formed an image of myself based on the thoughts in my mind, instead of the facts of why the divorce occurred- an image that would develop into very damaging attributes throughout my life.

Even as a young girl, I had a love for the Lord that I could not explain or understand. As I began to search for the love of an earthy father, the heavenly Father began to fill that emptiness with a love for Him, and by Him, that totally amazed me.

I recall in my teenage years feeling like the Lord was talking to me. One day, as I was running my bath, I heard a voice say, "You are going to marry a preacher." Years later, during my prayer time, I heard the voice again say, "I'm calling you to ministry." I did not tell anyone these words as I thought no one would have believed me but think I was crazy.

All I wanted to do was pray and spend time with God. I started working in the church with our youth, taught on Wednesday nights, and was very involved with the music department. I was also teaching pre-school at a Christian school in the area.

I had dated a guy when I was fifteen years old, and throughout the years, we had remained friends. My church was hosting Campmeeting services on Monday and Tuesday nights in May of 1991. One Monday night, I was in the choir, getting ready to sing, when I saw him come in . Something was different about him. I have heard people talk about love at first sight— but when I saw him that night, I thought that is the kind of guy I want to marry. I saw a love and passion in his spirit for God that I had not seen when we had dated before. I would find out later that God had called him into the ministry. We went out to dinner after the church service; I still remember what we were both wearing that night. I had on a navy dress with a white collar that buttoned up the front, with navy high heel shoes. He had on khaki slacks, light blue dress shirt, paisley tie, and navy sport coat. We went out again Tuesday night, Wednesday night, and, like the saying goes, the rest is history.

Two months later we were engaged, and March 21, 1992 we were married. The voice was right — I had married a preacher. Keith was amazing, so full of life. He was funny, very talented, and played any kind of instrument; and play them well too. He was handsome and had a last name I could pronounce, as it was always a fear of mine I would fall in love with someone whose last name I could not pronounce. Most important though, he made me the promise to never leave me like my dad had done. He promised to love me and stay with me forever. We were going to live happily ever after, working and serving the Lord. Three months after we were married, we accepted our first full- time positions in youth ministry.

In July 1995, God blessed us with our first child, Tyler, who looked just like his dad — big, blue eyes and a cute, little dimple. In October 1997, God blessed our family again with another son, Tanner, who looked just like me. He had big, brown eyes, so dark you could not tell where his pupil ended Our family was complete and life was perfect.

Two weeks before Tanner was born, Keith accepted his first pastoral position, but it did not take long for the honeymoon period to be over and trouble to start in the church. Standing at the back door one day, I remember hearing that all familiar voice. This time, these were not good words I heard: "There is an attack coming on your home to destroy it" were the words I heard so plainly that day. From that day forward, it felt like we fought every demon from hell. We learned to enjoy and cherish the good times, because they did not seem to last long. Keith and I loved each other and held on to the assurance that God had put us together, fighting with everything in us to keep our marriage strong.

We were the perfect couple in the eyes of people, a role model to younger couples, so we could not let others know we were having trouble in our marriage. Coming from a broken home, I was determined that my home would not end in divorce and my children would never have to go through the pain I had experienced.

In 2003, Keith and I were eleven years into marriage and ministry. I watched as the carefree, funny man I married slowly changed. I knew he was struggling to hold on to the calling on his life and the dreams deep inside of him, exhausted from blow after blow he had experienced from ministry and from people in the church.

I had been so wrapped up in being a mother, wife, and the perfect little pastor's wife that I had forgotten all the things for my life God had spoken to me about years ago .

It was on a Monday, in July 2003, when my life started down a road that would change me forever. It seemed as if someone flipped the light switch, because I had no idea what was going on in my body. I felt like I was choking when I tried to eat and lost thirty pounds in three months. I started having panic attacks. I can remember putting the boys to bed at night and saying to them, "Momma will see you in the morning," but that was for me, not them. I knew as long as I told my children that I would see them in the morning, I would have to live to see the morning. I went to the doctor, only to be told, "It's your sinuses. Take this medicine." The medicine did not help and the doctors did not try to find the reason for my health problems.

It was during this time that God started dealing with some major issues in my life, with insecurity and fear first on His list. Growing up, my sister and I never learned to swim because Mom was afraid we would drown. She was also afraid for us to ride a bike because she thought we would have a wreck. I did not have these kinds of fears, but if Keith was five minutes late coming home, I would go into a panic thinking something had happened to him. I did not want to pass fear onto my children, so God and I started to work. I was afraid that something bad was going to happen to me; not something that would kill me but something that would make me unable to care for myself.

When we would go out of town, I would watch for hospital signs on the interstate so I would know how to get to the nearest hospital. When I would feel these fears come over me, the only thing that brought relief would be to go into my bedroom and pray — exactly what God wanted — me with Him so we could work on freedom from these strongholds. As I look back now, I can see how God was preparing me for the valley of the shadow of death that would come years later. The old Kim needed to die so the new Kim could be prepared for the greater journey.

During this time, God started birthing intercessory prayer in my life. Intercessory prayer is praying on behalf of someone else or some certain issue to God. There were many nights I woke up at two or three in the morning with the feeling I needed to go and pray. Keith was very supportive during this time. There were times I would cook dinner, put it on the table, and say "I can't eat; I have to go pray." It was during this time God started to remind me of the gifts and calling He had placed on my life years ago.

On a Saturday night in February of 2004, while folding clothes, the Holy Spirit came on me so strong. I remember going to my knees and praying in the spirit. It was so different, and was literally a prayer language. I remember seeing the face of a beautiful, little girl. She had big, dark eyes and a round, little face. I knew she was from another country. The Lord spoke to me and said, "I have called you to the nations." I never said anything to anyone, not even Keith.

Something was slowing happening to me. I started feeling different, like I was being freed from the bonds of life that had held me captive for years. I would drop the boys off at school, get Keith off to the office, and go straight to my prayer closet. I would stay there for hours reading my Bible, praying, and worshiping, while listening to my praise-and-worship music. Many days I would set the alarm so that I would not be late picking the boys up from school. I felt different, and I longed to be free of every stronghold that had held me captive.

I will never forget one Sunday when the praise and worship started at church that I heard the Lord say, "Get out of your seat and go down front, and worship Me like you do in your prayer closet." I said, "Lord, you know how these people feel about praise and worship, and you want me to do what? You do remember I am the pastor's wife, and they will think I have gone nuts." He said, "Get out of your seat and go down front, and worship Me like you do in your prayer closet." I knew what I had to do... so I got out of my seat and went and stood in front of the first pew, and lifted my hands and started worshiping. There is such freedom in worship. It frees you from people's opinions and pride, and ushers you right to the feet of your Savior. Yes, it was hard that first Sunday, but it got easier each time.

KEITH AND I DECIDED TO LEAVE THE DENOMINATION with which we were affiliated in May of 2005. We were having problems in the church and had been praying and fasting, and we felt like God was saying, "Stand still." The leaders over us wanted us to move to another church. We shared with them that after fasting and praying, we felt like we needed to stay. However, they did not agree so they decided to remove us from pastoring the church. We were told we would not be going to another church. So, in one day we lost church, our income, and our home, because we lived in the church parsonage. I honestly believe this was the final blow for Keith and he never recovered from this blow.

We moved in with Keith's brother and sister-in-law, as we slowly tried to make sense of what had occurred. It is hard to recover from losing everything when you feel like you did what God was leading you to do.

We soon found a church to attend and slowing waited for the healing to begin. There were probably 600-700 people that attended this church. One of my cousins attended but we seldom saw each other. One Sunday though, we ended up sitting right in front of him. After the service, he said, "I need to tell you something but I don't want to upset you. Do you know who Allie is?" I said, "Yes, my grandmother from my dad's side of the family."

He said she died, and her funeral was that same day. I immediately turned to Keith and told him that I wanted to go to the funeral.

We sent the boys home with his brother and off we went to the funeral of my grandmother. I knew God had ordained my steps that morning, and it was not by coincidence that my cousin sat behind me that day.

We got to the funeral home, went in, and sat down on the pew with the cousins I knew. I glanced around, wondering which one was my dad. I finally turned to the cousin sitting beside me and asked, "Which one is my dad?" She pointed him out to me.

When the service was over, I got up, walked up to the pew where he was sitting, bent down beside him, and said, "You probably don't know who I am."

He said, "You are Kim."

"Yes, I just wanted to meet you and tell you I love you, and you have two grandsons." He told me he loved me too. I left the funeral home that day knowing what my dad looked like and knowing that God had ordained our meeting. God was bringing healing and restoration to this broken girl.

IN AUGUST OF 2006, KEITH AND I MOVED TO Morristown, Tennessee and planted a church. This was going to be a fresh start — a new beginning for our family. We found a building for the church, and the realtor who had helped us find the building was so inspired by our vision for the church that he paid our first month's rent on the building. We moved into a new condo and found schools for the boys. Life seemed good for the first time in years. Starting a church, Keith and I both knew we would have to find jobs until the church was established. Keith got his insurance license, while I got a job working as an administrative assistant in the education department at a local church. The boys formed friendships that they still have today and got involved in sports. It was a good life.

Remember in the previous chapter, I mentioned how God and I were working on major issues like insecurity and fear in me. Well, God had not forgotten. The insurance company Keith went to work for had their headquarters in Cincinnati, Ohio (you know where this is going). Yes, they sent him for training for a WEEK... a whole week. I knew the very minute he told me it was a test for me. I remember the boys and I taking him to the airport on Sunday afternoon. Inside, I was all to pieces but outside I was all smiles and strong. I know it sounds silly, but Keith was my safe place, my security. We had been married for fourteen years and had only spent maybe four nights apart, and that was when I was hospitalized for the birth of our sons. God was trying to teach me that my security was in Him and not anyone else — not even Keith — because He knew what was down the road in just four years and the lesson had to be learned quickly. After that trip, there were many more and I truly started to enjoy my time alone. Do not get me wrong' I loved Keith and missed him, but I could survive on my own with God.

In January of 2007, we were invited to be on TV in Atlanta, Georgia. I would be singing, and we would also be guest speakers. Two weeks before we received the invitation, while in my prayer time, I heard that all familiar voice tell me He was going to open a door of ministry for me in two weeks. It was exactly two weeks to the day that we received the email. I was supposed to do eight songs. We knew I needed to go into the studio and lay the tracks down for the songs. Keith played the piano, drums, and bass for the tracks. It was so much fun getting the music ready for the program.

The program went well, and by the eighth song, my nerves were mostly gone and I was just having fun. I got to share about intercessory prayer and God's faithfulness.

Things were going so well, and then came 2008. It was Christmas and I found out that Keith had reconnected on Facebook with a girl from his high school years. They were talking and communicating every day. She was posting very inappropriate things on his Facebook page, so I confronted him about it. At first, he denied everything but later admitted that something was going on between them. We went to counselling, and he apologized to the boys and me. I thought it was ended.

In 2009, we made the decision to close the church and work on our relationship. We wanted to get the boys involved in a church with a good youth group also, so we started attending a local church. Keith helped in the music department by playing the drums and preached on Sunday nights. He kept busy preaching at other area churches too.

In the summer of 2010, he was asked to come to Alabama and be the associate pastor/administrator for a pastor friend. Without any hesitation, he declined. He started declining all offers to preach. I knew something was not right, but he would not talk to me. He stopped all forms of affection toward me: no hand-holding, no touches, and not even an "I love you." I prayed and begged God to tell me what was going on, but no voice this time.

We were on our way to my sister's house, for Thanksgiving dinner, when he told me that after we finished dinner with my family, he and the boys would be leaving to go to his mom's house without me. I found out later the other woman and her children were at his mom's for Thanksgiving. After dinner, he and the boys left and were gone for five hours.

The following Tuesday, our oldest son had a wrestling match. Keith said his mom and stepdad were coming to the match. Keith was coming from work, so we took separate cars to the school. I called Keith when I got to the school to see if I needed to save his mom and stepdad a seat. He said that his stepdad was not coming and that a girl from his mom's church was bringing her to the match. I thought something was not right because I knew the church his mom went to, and most of the people were her age, not of the younger generation. I heard the voice I had learned to be my heavenly Father say to me, "If she is young, this is it." I went in, got a seat, and waited. Keith's mom came in; behind her was a blonde lady and her son, and behind her was Keith. The voice said these three words to me. "THIS IS IT." They sat on the opposite side of the gym. He finally made his way to where I was sitting. I greeted him with, "Is that your girlfriend? She's pretty." He denied that anything was going on and told me I was making everything up.

The next day, God told me to go on a three-day fast. That night after dinner, Keith said he needed to talk to me. I sat down on the bed to listen and with three sentences, my world fell apart. He said,

"I saw an attorney today and I have filed for a divorce. I have transferred my job to the office in Johnson City. I am leaving Saturday and moving in with my mom." I remember telling him I would never sign divorce papers. If this is what he wanted, he would do it all. I left and went to a friend's house where she prayed and talked with me. I called my mom and told her and a few close friends. I was so numb and in shock that it just did not seem real. I remember walking back into the house that night, and he was asleep on the couch. I climbed into bed and cried. *How can this be happening to me? He promised me he would not leave me like my dad. What did I do wrong?*

While talking with my friend the night before, she had expressed to me that when I felt the emotion of angry rising up inside me, I needed to find some way to get it out. She suggested getting in the car and while I was driving to yell or scream.

I had dropped the boys off at school the next morning and was praying on the way home. By the time I walked through the front door of our house, I was screaming at the devil. I knew this was an attack from hell to break my family apart, and I was mad. I went down the hall to my bedroom, yelling, "I hate you, devil." I reach the bedroom and pick up a plastic coat hanger and began hitting the dresser, screaming, "I hate you, devil." When I came to myself, I was on the floor sobbing.

I prayed but all I heard was "Trust Me and love Keith unconditionally." Saturday came, and Keith moved out. The boys were still with me because school was not out for winter break yet. I remember going into the bathroom and started laughing, because he had taken the wrong toothbrush. He took mine instead of his, so he really had not gotten away from me. He just took me with him.

On Sunday, the boys informed me they were going to go live with their dad. I found out from the school that he had already told the school the boys would be transferring and had talked to the coaches at the new school about their sports. When you think your heart cannot break into any more pieces, it can. Pain is real, and no amount of saying it is not does not change the fact. December 15th, I was served divorce papers; and December 26th, my boys left to live with their dad.

I cannot even begin to describe the loneliness and emptiness I was feeling. I still don't know what kept me from losing my mind except for God. God kept me for you: You reading this book right now; you, the woman whose marriage fell apart today; you, the mother whose children walked away today. He kept me alive and in my right mind just for you.

The first thing I had to do was decide where to live. Was I to stay in Morristown or move to Johnson City where my family lived? I also had to get a job because I had been able to stay home and not work for about a year at that time. My sister offered for me to come and live with her until I could get on my feet. So, I was moving to Johnson City. I got a job working for the hospital and started living minute by minute. Sometimes you cannot go day by day or even hour by hour; you just go minute by minute.

Work became my outlet. I worked from 7:00 am –3:30 pm daily. I would go to bed around 8:30, so I just had a few hours to deal with life. However, I was struggling one day about what to do. I did not have the money to get an attorney, but God had told me not to do anything at the moment. I received a call from a minister who was also a close friend. He said he was praying for me that day, asking God to help me do the right thing and make the right decisions. He said God told him that I was doing exactly what He told me to do.

Keith started letting me have the boys every other weekend and every Wednesday. I loved my time with my boys and missed them. My boys and I had always been close, and I could not make any sense of why they were turning away from me too.

In March, I was finally able to save enough money to move out and get a place of my own. It was so nice having a place I could call my own. Here, I could close the door and fall apart, and no one would know.

April 2011: I was at work when I saw the girl from the wrestling match. I did not know she had gotten a job at the same place. She was pregnant, so I knew then what was going on : My husband was having an affair, and she was pregnant with his child.

I am so grateful that God revealed piece by piece of this puzzle to me. I could not have handled the whole puzzle at one time. He would reveal one piece, and we (God and me) would deal with it. God would then let me rest for a bit, and then we would deal with another piece. After seeing her that day at work, God said it is time to get an attorney now.

When I worked at the church in Morristown, there was one of the small group leaders in our department that was an attorney. I called him and he took my case.

In July, the baby was born; that was reality day. I went to Alabama and stayed with my best friend and her family for several days. I cannot tell you why I have gone through what I have and survived, except to tell you to hold on. You may feel like you cannot go another step, but just know God will not leave you. If you have started through, He will walk you to the end. I promise He will not leave you to die in the middle of the storm. Hold on, my friend. He has the end already in sight; just keep holding His hand and let Him walk you to the end.

It is indescribable pain to know that the person you trusted with your life to love and protect you until death has been with another woman and conceived a child with her. I wanted to die. I went to bed asking God, "Please just let me go to sleep and not wake up," only to wake up and get mad at God. I also found out during this time that my boys were calling her Mom and they started calling me Kim.

Christmas 2011: I ordered some videos from the Discovery and History Channels for the boys to give their dad for Christmas. I came out from work one day, not long after Christmas, to find these videos under my car. The other woman had gotten upset because I had bought these for the boys to give their dad and had thrown them under my car. After this, all contact stopped with

Keith and my boys. January 2012 would be the last time I would see my children. Keith knew I did not have the funds to take him to court to fight for the boys.

There are two memories I will cherish until the day I die of my Papaw during this time of my life. After contact with the boys stopped, I remember going into his house, crawling into his lap, and just crying and crying as he held me. Yes, me, a forty-two-year-old woman crawled up in her eighty-nine-year-old Papaw's lap crying.

The second happened several months later. It had been months since I had seen or talked with the boys, and I was struggling just to stay alive. I started to leave Papaw's house, and he took my hand and said these words to me, "You know your mom and I love you, and we would do anything for you, but you are the only one who can pull yourself out of this. If you do not, you're going to lose your mind and that's exactly what they want to happen to you." Then he started praying for me out loud. "Do not ever let the devil make you think you are all alone. You are not alone."

By this time, I was so tired of the pain that I was angry. I was angry at God. *Why was He allowing this to happen to me? What did I do? He had the affair and the baby with the other woman, so why was I the one suffering? Why was I the one losing everything while he went on with his life with another woman and my children?* I stopped going to church. I stopped praying and reading my Bible also. I was ANGRY!!!

I was struggling just to survive; this went on from January until early May 2012. I don't know why but I texted a pastor friend in Morristown that I knew had church services on Saturday to see what time it started. I made myself go. I was so numb and could not feel anything. Every time I wanted to give up and quit, something inside would not let me. I know now it was God holding on and loving me when I could not hold on anymore. There is nothing, nothing, like the love of God our Father.

Pastor Kyle was preaching that Saturday service. He stopped right in front of me and said, "God is bringing you through what you've been going through so you can help someone who is getting ready to start going through the same thing." I went home that day and, for the first time in months, I cried. I picked up my Bible and begin to read. Nothing major happened, but for the first time in months I had hope that I was going to be all right.

It was July 2012, and the date was scheduled to sign the divorce papers. I called the attorney and told him I was not ready to sign, so we rescheduled for August. I decided to go to North Carolina and talk with a pastor friend and his wife. I shared with them about my state of mind and how angry I was at God. The pastor shared with me that on Friday, they would be fasting for me that God would bring breakthrough. I agreed to fast with them.

Their church was having Campmeeting in August, so I took my vacation and went up for the Campmeeting I had been out shopping on Thursday and was driving back to their home when I felt the presence of the Lord in a way I had not felt in a long time. I began to pray in the spirit. That night at church, the evangelist called me out and said, "The devil is shaking because he knows he's going to have to give back to you everything he has stolen from you; and not just give it back, but give it back seven times."

I had planned on staying through Sunday with the pastor and his wife, but I had a strong feeling I needed to go back home and go to my church on Sunday. After the service on Sunday, I knew why I had returned. The pastor preached on Jesus the Restorer. He said, "There are some of you that the devil is going to have to give your stuff back and give it back seven times." I knew he was confirming what God had told me on Thursday night. He said, "Some of you are afraid to embrace the new things God has for you because you are afraid to let go of the old."

I was scheduled to sign the divorce papers the next day, and God knew I needed confirmation from Him to sign. I signed the divorce papers the next day, which was August 20, 2012 almost two years after Keith had filed. I knew in my spirit I had done everything possible to get my family back, and I could lay my head down at night and go to sleep having peace about it. I had fought with everything in me to save my marriage, but it was time to let go. I did not know what was going to happen next in my life, but I had the assurance that I was in the palm of God's hand and He was guiding my steps.

I started going to North Carolina on the weekends to spend time with my friends and go to church with them. They talked with me about moving to North Carolina and, after much prayer, I felt like God said, "Do it." I started putting in resumes but no job was made available. In October, I decided I would quit my job in Tennessee and start making preparation for the move. God told me to go on my first forty-day fast. Two weeks into the fast, I had a job and an apartment within an hour in North Carolina. I moved on

November 10, 2012 and started the new journey. In January, I was offered a promotion with a $2.00 an hour raise. Restoration had started, and God had proven true to His word.

During all this time, I had stepped away from doing anything that had to do with ministry. In January of 2013, the music minister asked if I would start singing specials. I agreed; it was not easy because it had been over two years since I had sung, but God had been faithful to me and I wanted to please Him. In March, the music minister came back and asked if I would join the worship team. Slowly, God was placing me right back where I was before the divorce. On March 17, 2013, I received a text asking if I would speak at a ladies conference in April in Tennessee. This would be the first time I would be giving my testimony, and I wanted to share my heart, but I did not want to disrespect Keith. I immediately started praying and fasting about the conference. While praying one day, God showed me a vision of myself praying for a lady. I knew it was a pastor's wife, but I did not know the lady in the vision.

When I arrived to speak at the conference, I learned that the other speaker was the wife of a pastor in the area. I had never seen her before, and I had forgotten about the vision until the host of the conference asked if the speakers would have prayer with the ladies who had attended. When I turned to say something to the other speaker, God immediately reminded me of the vision. I told her that I had to pray for her first. I told her what God had showed me in the vision and the words He had spoken to me that day about her.

I am so glad we serve a God that is faithful to keep His word and promises. When I got home that night, I just sat in total amazement of the wonders of our God. I picked up my journal to write about the day's events, and God started speaking to me about things ahead. One thing He spoke was that He was going to send me to places I had never been to before. I would ask how they had heard about me. The next week, I was having lunch with a co-worker when I received a text from my best friend in Tennessee, asking me if I would speak at her hairdressers' mother-and-daughter banquet. It was to be held in a church I had never heard of before. In June, the lady I had prayed for at the conference called to see if I would come and speak at her church. God is faithful to His calling. Just because your life falls apart and you think it's over doesn't mean it's over in God's eyes. When God calls you to do a ministry for Him, He will protect His calling on your life.

One of the hardest things has been not seeing my boys or having any communication with them. Holidays, birthdays, and Mother's Day are the worse. Doing a mother/daughter banquet, knowing that the next day was Mother's Day and I would not be seeing the children I had given birth to (and they would be spending it with the woman they call Mom who had broken my home) was almost more than I could handle. I had tried to act like everything was fine, being all smiles on the outside, but only God and I knew the war going on inside of me.

I had started doing a little thing of texting God messages to my own number. (I told you we would roll our eyes at things in the book... so, go ahead; here is a good opportunity.) I was on my way home from church that day when I texted God and asked him if he would send me a Mother's Day gift. It had been a hard day, but I made it through and was very thankful when it was bedtime. The next day when I got home from work, a flower, balloons, and a card from my friend in Alabama were sitting by my front door. I called her to thank her, and she said she just felt like sending me a Mother's Day gift because she knew it was going to be a bad day for me. God had sent me my Mother's Day gift through my friend that I had asked of Him.

When Father's Day came, I remember thinking that I did not know how to get in touch with my dad. I knew the pain I had felt on Mother's Day not being with my children, and I did not want to cause pain like that to my father. Before the divorce, my dad and I had been talking about getting together so he could meet the boys, but when things happened, I lost contact with him. On July 3, 2013, I received a call from my dad. He told me he had a new phone number and if I wanted to call him back, he would like to hear from me. There was no hesitation; I knew God had given me this opportunity and I was walking through this door. That night we talked for a long time. I found out I had four aunts one who had passed away from cancer. I learned he was in the army before he and mom were married. I was able to, for the first time in life, call my dad on his birthday, Thanksgiving, and Christmas, and say I love you.

A few months later we had dinner together. I will always remember the words of a friend who said, "God promised you he would restore what the devil had stolen. Why would He not go back to the first thing the devil stole and start there?" How true. The little girl who had searched all her life for the love of her earthly father was experiencing a relationship with the missing piece for the first time.

I wish I could tell you I never doubted God and I skipped along the path laid with rose peddles, but that would be a lie. The hardest part for me is the waiting. There came a time about three-and-a-half years into this new journey of divorced life that I started doubting everything I had lived in my Christian life. I had thoughts of, *Is any of this really real? Did God really speak these things to me, or did I make them up to make myself feel better in the rough times?*

What about this one... Why pray? Why ask God for anything else? Nothing has changed. I have not seen the things He's promised happen yet so why ask Him to do anything else? I tried to read my Bible, but nothing spoke to me. I found myself falling into a pit that I knew I would never get out of on my own. It was like I could feel the dirt covering me. I was dying, slowly bleeding to death, and no one knew or could help me.

It had been two years since I had seen the boys or spent time with them. I missed hearing their voices, their laughs, and hugging them. I just missed them. Their cell numbers had been changed, and I could not get their new numbers from anyone. I sent cards, only to have them returned with nasty messages on them. I hated holidays because they were just a reminder of everything I had lost and that I was alone.

I listened to the enemy say, "How can you get up and sing about the Lord when you are struggling about whether all this is real or not? You are a fake."

So, I told the music minister that I needed to step down and take a break, because I was struggling with some things. She agreed to let me step down from singing special, but she kept me on the worship team once a month. She said, "if I let you quit both, you will end up quitting church."

It was also during this time that the devil sent a trap I never thought I would fall into. I found myself being tempted in the same area that had destroyed my marriage. I was so lonely during this time, and I felt like the promises from God about restoring my family and the love of a mate were never going to happen. So I decided Kim was going to be happy, laugh again, and enjoy life no matter the consequences. It started very innocently, but I can tell you that if the devil is in it – it is not innocent. The guy was married. It simply started by texting and talking; within weeks, it was completely out of control. Even though nothing sexual ever happened, I knew what I was doing was wrong but I was happy. Sin will take you down a road you never thought you would walk down and take from you more than you ever wanted to give up. I was now the other woman I had cried so many tears over for breaking up my family.

I am so glad that God still protects us, even when we are walking down a path we know is wrong. Sometimes I wonder if it is us He's protecting or the seed of His promise inside of us. What you are going through right now is not about you; it is about someone you will come into contact with down the road that needs to hear your story.

I believe God exposed things in the relationship before anything sexual happened. I know this because even though I had walked away from God and was in disobedience, He still warned me. I was sitting in my chair on Friday night, watching TV. We were texting back and forth, when I heard God say, "You have seventy-two hours to stop this or I will expose everything." I just pushed the words away; I was having fun and I was happy. Tuesday morning, God started exposure. It is hard for us to accept pain from a heavenly Father, but His word tells us He disciplines those He loves.

I had made the decision to walk this path knowing it was wrong, and now I had to face the consequences of my decision.

WHEN EVERYTHING WAS EXPOSED, I LOST EVERY-thing again. I lost my job, friends, church, and now I lived in a state two and half hours away from the family and the only friends who had not turned their backs on me. I promised the guy I would protect him and take all the blame, so now I was alone again.

Having only one income, and then losing that income, is not a good situation. I had brought a new car nine days before all this happened. I was putting resumes in everywhere and could not get a job anywhere. I had applied for unemployment, but it had not been approved yet. I was talking to my mom on the phone one day when she said, "You know, if you would get on your knees and repent, God will turn this around quickly." I wanted to shake her, and not in a good way. I knew she was telling me the truth, but I was not ready.

After seven weeks, the black hole came in July. There was still no job; unemployment had not started; what little money I had saved was gone. I had never been one to take much medication, so there was not any "strong" medication in the cabinet. I went to the store and brought some over-the-counter sleeping pills. I knew I had created the mess I was living in now. It was all my fault; I felt hopeless and helpless. I wondered what other people were saying about me, what they were thinking. I was the other woman and was just like the woman who broke up my home.

I sat down and wrote letters to my boys, telling them how much I still loved them. While writing the letters, I heard the words, "You can take the whole bottle, but it doesn't mean you will die."

My mom also called while I was writing the letters. She said, "I have been worried about you, so I called some friends to have them pray for you. I told them I was afraid you might do something to hurt yourself."

She said that one of them said, "Well, she could take a whole bottle of pills but that doesn't mean she would die." I held the bottle in my hand, knowing nothing was going to happen because God wasn't finished with me. I also knew I had to turn from the path I was on and surrender to God's will for my life.

Sometimes all you can see is the ruined pieces of your life lying around you, but God sees the beautiful masterpiece hanging on the wall in the gold frame. He knows how it is all going to work out. All He needs is for us to trust Him. We might not like the way things are in our lives right now, but that is the awesome part about God: He lives in the beginning, middle, and end. He knows how it is going to work out.

Saturday night, I was sitting in my chair, watching TV, when I heard that voice say, "Get up in the morning and drive to Tennessee and go to church." I really did not want to go to church, but I obeyed. That day, I started on the road of healing and restoration again.

The next week, I was out looking for a job when I suddenly started to cry. When I got home, I went through the door and enter my bedroom sobbing. I knelt on my knees right there in my bedroom and asked God to forgive me for the things I had done.

The more time I spent in prayer and studying His word, the more He reminded me that the promises and the book you are holding in your hands right now still needed to be completed. You may think the choices of your life have voided the plans God has for you, but they are only delays; only another chapter in your life that someone needs to hear. God's promises and plans for your life are Yea and Amen. He doesn't change His mind and walk away just because you have a bad day and fail. His love never changes. He loves you as much today as He will tomorrow!!

Friday, September 26, 2014, after my prayer time, I felt an urge to get my journal. I knew the Lord wanted to talk with me, and I needed to write some things down. The thought did cross my mind, "Lord, I have books full of things I thought you had told me that I am still waiting on to happen," but I got the pen and started writing. The word I heard was RESTORATION!!!!

Restoration had been spoken over me three times by three different ministers, and now again He was saying, "I have not forgotten one promise I have made to you. Restoration is coming, even though you do not believe it." He also laid on my heart a heaviness to finish the book.

When my eyes opened the next day, I knew I needed to go to Dominion Life Church in Morristown, Tennessee the following Sunday. It was a three-hour drive, but I knew I had to be there.

When I walked through the door, I knew God was ordering my steps. The presence of the Lord was so strong in the place. If you are familiar with the Pentecostal ways, you know what the term "read my mail" means. It is when God uses someone who knows nothing about what's going on in your life to confirm what He has spoken to you. Well, my mail was read... RESTORATION was the word that day. God confirmed that I would minister to hurting people that needed to hear my story, and then God asked me this question... "Where's the book?" This reminded me of God asking Adam in the garden if he had eaten from the tree. God already knew where the book was; it was tucked way under the bed. God said, "Complete the book."

> I felt very strongly that I needed to pay my tithes. I was only drawing unemployment because I still had not found a job. I was not going to church anywhere at the time, so I did not have a church to give my tithes. I got the money out of my purse and handed it to the pastor's wife.

> When I did, she looked at me with wide eyes and said, "I saw in the spirit a lock and when you handed me the money, there was a key that unlocked the lock." Within two weeks, I got a part-time job at Lifeway Christian bookstore. I started the week my unemployment was due to stop. You can call it whatever you want, but I call it a "God

moment." I found a church in North Carolina and started attending. God had been true to His promises again, and this time I was determined to hold on to God.

ALTHOUGH THESE WERE SOME OF THE HARDEST times financially, I look back and this was one of the most peaceful and enjoyable times in my life. I know that probably sounds crazy, but God was taking care of me. Let me explain. When I was working full-time, I was bringing home around $2,000 a month. When I lost my job, I went down to only drawing around $800 on unemployment. When the unemployment ended, I began working part-time, making $7.00 a hour working 25 hours a week. I never went without anything. All the bills were always paid. I do not know how except God. I learned I could depend on God to supply my every need.

Sometimes you may think God is taking everything away from you, but He's only teaching you to trust Him. He is Jehovah-Jireh... My provider. I know Him as my healer, my need supplier, my love, my safety. When He becomes your EVERYTHING, then you will want for NOTHING. Learn to trust Him now; fall into His arms and say, "Lord, I surrender my will to You. Help me trust You with the plan You have for my life." I promise you; it is better than you can imagine.

There came a time when the car insurance was due, and I did not have the money. I did not say anything to anyone; I just prayed. Sunday came and I did not go to church because my funds were low, and I knew I needed to save my gas in the car to get to work the next week. After church, a couple from the church called and asked if they could come over that afternoon. After we had visited for a while and they started to leave, she handed me an envelope. She told me that another couple from church I had met through them asked if they would get this to me. They left, and I opened the envelope and found a check for the amount I needed for the car insurance. It was not until the next day on my way to pay the insurance that I knew God had orchestrated this to be the day and time to be in the car.

As I was driving, I heard this story on the radio. A mother was giving her testimony of going through a divorce and her daughter being turned against her through lies. She said for years she had prayed for God to reveal the truth to her daughter and restore their relationship. Then one day, she received a call from her daughter, who was crying and begging for her forgiveness. She explained to her mother that God had showed she had been lied to about her mom.

I remember thinking, God, this isn't about me paying my car insurance; it's about me hearing this story on the radio today. He wanted me in the car on Monday at noon to let me know if He restored one broken relationship, He would do the same for my boys and me. I must not give up hope.

A FEW DAYS BEFORE CHRISTMAS IN 2014, I NEEDED hairspray so I decided I would stop at Walmart on my way home from work. I can literally see this while writing this book. I heard that voice telling me to buy Keith and his new wife a Christmas card and send it to them. I said to myself, "I know that wasn't God." I thought, *I'm not going after hairspray now; I'm going home*, but I heard that voice again say, "I told you to buy a Christmas card and send it to them."

I thought, *Ok, if I can find a parking place close, then I'll do it*. I turned up the aisle, and the second spot was empty.

I heard the voice say, "Get a card that says to a wonderful family at Christmas."

I thought, *Lord, You are really stretching me*. I walked in the door, and, no joke, right in front of the door was a card stand with a card that said "To a wonderful family at Christmas."

I said, "Ok God, I'll get it." I put the card in my hand and thought, *If they don't have my hairspray, then I'm not standing in line for just a card*, but I was going to stand in line for just one can of hairspray.

They had my hairspray so to the checkout I went, with the card and the hairspray. I got to the checkout and that voice said, "Buy a gift card for them to go out to dinner."

By this time, I was not a happy camper at all. I got to the checkout, threw this stuff down, and the girl checking me out said, "How's your day going?"

I told her not really well because the Lord was having me buy my ex-husband and his new wife a Christmas card and gift card to send them. I thought she would have sympathy for me, but oh no. She said, "If God's telling you to do that, then you really need to do it."

I got home and literally cried the whole time I was fixing the card. Things had finally settled down and I just didn't want them to start up again. I remember begging God, "Please don't let things start up again. Please God, don't let them start harassing me again." I fixed the card and mailed it the next day, thinking, *Now I will wait to see if the fireworks would start again.*

A few days later, God started dealing with me about apologizing to the family of the husband with whom I had the relationship with. I sat down and wrote a letter to her, asking her forgiveness for disrespecting her and her family by crossing the line with her husband.

In mid-January of 2015, I had been praying and studying, and I felt like I needed to get my writing pad and pen. This time I knew I was supposed to write a letter to my boys. I remember pouring my heart out in the letter to them. I told them how sorry I was that I did not react the way that I should have during their divorce. I told them I wished I could go back and handle things differently, but I was hurting so bad I just didn't know how to react. I told them I missed them and still love them, that there was nothing I wanted more than a relationship with them again.

After pouring my heart out to the boys and asking them for their forgiveness and understanding, God said, "It's time to ask Keith for forgiveness." I remember thinking, *God, do you remember he's the one that had the affair, not me? Shouldn't he be asking me for forgiveness?*

God said, "I told you to ask him to forgive you for holding hard feelings and unforgiveness in your heart toward him." I got through the letter, breathed a deep breath, and knew there was one more thing I needed to do. I wrote to the other woman. "I thank you for taking care of my boys while I have not been there with them. I prayed blessings and many happy years of marriage for you and Keith." I finished the letter, and for the first time since December of 2010, I felt free.

Two weeks later, I felt like I needed to send the boys some money. I was not sure if they would get it or even keep it, but I knew it was something I needed to do. About two weeks later, on a Friday morning, my phone went off and it was a text from Keith. It had been three years since I had heard from him. He said he was texting just to see if I was alright. We texted back and forth for hours, just chatting and catching up on things. Shocked is an understatement for what I was feeling, but for the first time since 2010, we were being human and civil with each other.

It had been a year since everything had happened. I was still living in North Carolina, working the part-time job at Lifeway.

God had been so faithful, meeting every need during the last year. May's payment was due for the car insurance. I did not have the money, and this time it was not coming. In North Carolina, there is a law that you must have insurance on your car.

When the insurance was cancelled because I had not been able to make the payment, the cancellation was reported to the state. I received a letter from the DMV office. I called to explain about losing my full-time job and only having a part-time job, trying to plead my case with them. I've always believed and stood for total honesty so when I was asked, "Ma'am, did you drive the car to get to work knowing you did not have insurance?" my answer was "Yes, I did." I received a letter the next week saying I would have to park the car and turn in my tag because of the violation of driving without insurance.

What am I going to do? I kept thinking, *I told the truth, and now I can't drive my car.*

My mom kept saying, "Maybe it's time for you to come back to Tennessee."

Moving back to Johnson City, Tennessee was the last thing I wanted to do in my life.

I had prayed for weeks before all this started, "Lord, put me where You want me, with whom You want me with, and doing what You want me to do." Now would I accept what He wanted for my life? I finally surrendered and said, "Ok, Lord, if You want me to leave North Carolina and move back to Tennessee, that's what I will do."

I talked with the manager at Lifeway and asked about transferring to the store in Johnson City. He gave me the OK to speak to the manager in Johnson City and, no surprise, they had an opening. With the referral from the manager in North Carolina, I was hired for the same position.

Now where was I going to live and how was I going to move from North Carolina to Tennessee? I went to Tennessee and found a one-bedroom apartment at the complex where I lived before moving to North Carolina, but it would not be ready until July 10th. I was scheduled to start my job at Lifeway in Johnson City on June 29th. I had no other choice but to live with my mom for two weeks until I could move into the apartment. Moving day was scheduled for Saturday, June 27th. I had the money for the first month's rent on the apartment. My cousin was coming from Tennessee to North Carolina to drive the truck for me, and co-workers from Lifeway were helping me pack the truck on Friday. I needed the money for the truck and for a storage building to store my things for two weeks. I had changed my address, my driver's license, car registration, and insurance for the car in Tennessee. I turned in my North Carolina car tag so all was clear.

I called a friend and asked if she would be able to help with the money to cover the U-Haul truck, but I did not say anything about needing more money for the storage building. She agreed without any hesitation. It was Friday morning, packing day, when the money came in for the truck. There was more than I had expected. It was exactly to the penny, and I mean the penny, for what I needed for the truck and the storage building. I called my friend and said,

"How did you know I needed more money?" She said, "I felt like I needed to send that exact amount," so I told her what had happened. I knew for some reason God was closing the door for me in North Carolina and opening one in Tennessee. I had exactly what I needed to the penny to pay for moving expenses.

After being in Tennessee for a few days, I received a call from one of my cousins. His secretary had a friend who worked at the hospital in management. They were hiring, and she wanted to know if I would be interested in a job. I filled out the application and was hired for the job. I started full-time with benefits on July 28th, exactly one month after I moved back to Tennessee. I was now living in my own apartment with a full-time job. God had directed my steps back for this new journey.

SITTING HERE, WRITING THIS BOOK, I'M OVER-
whelmed with emotions thinking about God's faithfulness toward
me. You might be thinking that it's all over; you might feel like
you're down for the count, but God's not finished with you. You
will get up and witness the faithfulness and the keeping power of
an almighty God. He is not done with you! Shake yourself! Get
up, child of God, and see what God's getting ready to do for you.
If He kept me, He will certainly keep you. You can count on God
to keeping every promise He's made to you.

Summer of 2016, I was relaxing by the pool on a Saturday when I received a text from Keith. He told me that the transmission had gone out in Tyler's car. There was still no communication between the boys and me, but I knew immediately in my spirit I needed to reach out to help Tyler with his car. I knew I had to contact him myself. I could not go through letting anyone else give him this money — it had to go from my hand to his hand. The only thing about him I knew was where he was working, and I really did not want to go to his work to give him the money. I was not sure what his reaction would be when he saw me, and a public scene was the last thing I wanted for either one of us.

Afraid about this, I put a fleece out before God and asked Him if this was really what I was supposed to do. The fleece was answered, and off I went to take the money to Tyler. I remember being sick to my stomach and praying, "God, please don't let there be a scene."

Still not knowing what kind of reaction I would receive, I walked in the door and there my son stood. He saw me and a half-smile came across his face. I knew in my heart God was directing these steps.

I walked up to him and said, "I'm not here to cause any trouble, but your dad told me the transmission went out in your car, and I wanted to give you some money to get it fixed." I handed him the money and he thanked me. I said, "You look great. Can I give you a hug?" He said "Yes." I hugged my son for the first time in four years.

I said, "I love you and tell Tanner I love him too." By the time I got to the car, I lost it. There were so many emotions I was feeling at that time. I knew God had worked a miracle, and my steps had been directed by Him. Healing was taking place and restoration between my children had begun.

So, ten years later, I am still standing, standing stronger, standing happy and content with my life. I am standing only because of a love from my heavenly Father who proved to be all I needed. He proved that I could trust Him, He would never walk away.

So, to the woman whose home and marriage have just fallen apart; to the woman whose heart is broken because your children have walked away; to the young girl missing the father in her life; to the woman who's angry and mad at life, HOLD ON. In the name of Jesus, I speak restoration over your life. It's not over. Fall into the arms of a loving father who wants to love all the hurt away, love all the wounds and the scars from life away. He loves you. You mean so much to Him that He spared my life. He kept me alive so I could write this book and let you know that if He did it for me, He will do it for you. He loves you that much.

I cannot wait to hear your story of restoration. I look forward to hearing the good things that God has done in your life. Until we meet again, love and hugs.

Kim